W9-BTM-998

inside
dunder mifflin

The Ultimate Fan's Guide to The Office

inside
dunder mifflin

The Ultimate Fan's Guide to The Office

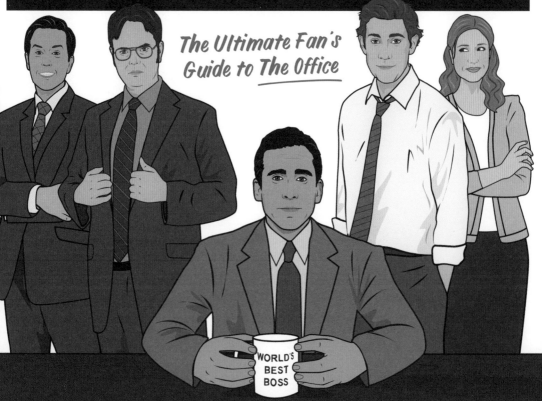

WORLD'S BEST BOSS

Smith Street Books

Amy Lewis

Illustrations by
Chantel de Sousa

AMOUNT DUE
$88.94

Please Forgive me!

WELCOME TO
Dunder Mifflin

When *The Office* made its debut on screens in 2005, the NBC network could not have predicted the show's worldwide success and future status as one of the most popular sitcoms in television history. Based on the acclaimed BBC comedy of the same name, written by Ricky Gervais and Stephen Merchant, many critics believed that an American version of *The Office* wouldn't work because the humor was simply too British and too subtle for American audiences.

Apart from the occasional gem like *Seinfeld* and *Arrested Development*, which focussed on clever writing and playing the long game when it came to setting up a joke, the mainstream American sitcom landscape at the time was vastly different from what it is today. The most popular sitcoms in the US were usually centered around the family unit, utilizing a small home-styled set and a built-in laugh track. *The Office* had no laugh track, leaving us plenty of space and time to shuffle awkwardly in our seats when Michael Scott's bad jokes bombed. The documentary-style format allowed us to see how the characters behaved when they thought they were being filmed as well as when they thought they weren't.

Like its UK counterpart, the show used relatively unknown actors in the cast to make the documentary format more believable to audiences. The fundamental elements were the same – a small-town paper company trying to stay in business in an increasingly paperless world. Scranton in Pennsylvania was chosen as the home of Dunder Mifflin because of its similarities to Slough, the setting of the UK version of the show. Scranton is to New York City as Slough is to London – far smaller and anything but glamorous.

The Office rated well across its nine seasons, but didn't break any records. Its success can best be measured in terms of the hordes of viewers attracted to repeats of the show on streaming services, and those of us who will happily binge-watch the show forever. There is something so comforting about turning on *The Office*, even just as background noise after a long day. It's hard to imagine a time when Michael Scott, Dwight Schrute, Pam Beesly and Jim Halpert weren't a part of our lives.

This book has been written as a tribute to the employees of Dunder Mifflin, who we got to know so well over the 201 episodes of *The Office*.

MICHAEL SCOTT'S
guide to business

0188451

Date _____ 20___

M _____

No. _____

Reg. No.	Clerk	ACCOUNT FORWARD	
1			
2			
3			
4			

What are your thoughts on the future of the paper industry, given the advances in technology we've seen in the past ten years?

People ask me, "Michael, how do you do it? How do you manage a branch of a highly successful paper company while we advance towards a world that doesn't need paper?" I say, forget about the product. I'm not here to sell paper. That's not what Dunder Mifflin is about. I'm here to build a family ... and sell paper.

What is the most important thing you can do to retain a customer's business?

You need to be their friend. No, you need to be their *best* friend. One of my biggest clients is an elementary school principal. He works about 60 hours a week and has four kids of his own. Widower. When he runs out of paper, he calls me up. Do I take his order immediately and fulfill it? No, I do not. I like the personal touch. I usually show up around 4 pm on a Friday, unannounced. Take him out for a slice of pizza and a couple of brewskies.

I take his order by hand, at the table. That's personal service. He tried to order on the website last month. I've canceled the order and I'm heading out to the school this afternoon with a basket of muffins and a six pack.

What is the next technological advance that will revolutionize the paper industry?

I think it's printers. I have a dream that every home in America will have a printer in each room. Families will be connected by printing. Printers will be connected to each other on the internet. When a printer runs out of paper, it will be able to go online, phone up a Dunder Mifflin branch and order more paper for itself. That's the future I want to live in.

What do you do in your spare time?

I invent stuff. I was always dropping things in the toilet at work. My phone, my wallet, coffee mugs. So I invented the "Toilet Buddy." It's a net that you hang in the toilet. It catches things before they fall in the water. Then you just reach in and grab them out.

THE ULTIMATE OFFICE PRANK GUIDE
with Jim Halpert

When you have to work with someone like Dwight, the only way to get through your day is to spend at least 90 percent of it making his life a misery. Given that I can usually get most of my job done in the first 45 minutes of the day, I've got plenty of time to focus on just this.

Dwight's desk space is very important to him. I like to get in a couple of hours early for work and move his desk. Sometimes I've come in on a Sunday to move it – that's only when it's somewhere really difficult to get it to, like the roof. As for my favorite desk locations, they are probably the ones where I've really thought outside of the box. I once moved his desk and computer inside the men's room. It took me a couple of hours to saw the end off the desk so it would be short enough to fit inside the cubicle but it was worth it.

I also like to time Dwight in the bathroom. I compile a report at 5 pm each day of all of his visits and their duration. I then place this on a letterhead I made up for a security company, attention it to "Regional Manager: Dunder Mifflin" and copy him in. The fax goes to Dwight and Dunder Mifflin corporate at 5.30 pm every night. It takes about an hour of my time each day but, as you can imagine, it is totally worth it.

One time I photocopied a paperclip onto 200 sheets of copy paper and filled the printer tray with them. Every time Dwight would print or photocopy, a paperclip would appear in the same place on every page. Then I watched as Dwight pulled the entire photocopier apart, getting angrier and angrier. Must have taken him a whole afternoon to take it apart. And it only cost Dunder Mifflin $1100 to replace it.

Despite being only six episodes long and initially receiving mixed reviews, the first season of *The Office* is packed with laughs and sets the scene for the characters who audiences grew to love. Via a mock documentary format, we meet the team at Scranton paper company Dunder Mifflin, led by branch manager Michael Scott. Michael's enthusiasm for blurring the lines between his personal and professional life is matched only by his complete lack of self-awareness. This, along with an ongoing rivalry between salesmen Dwight Schrute and Jim Halpert, frequently results in bedlam around the office. We also get an insight into the unspoken romantic connection between Jim Halpert and the receptionist Pam Beesly, who we learn is enduring the third year of her engagement to rugged but inconsiderate Roy Anderson from the warehouse.

In *Diversity Day*, Michael's problematic Chris Rock impersonation leads to HR intervention. This in turn results in Michael running his own training on diversity and descending even deeper into political incorrectness. In *Basketball*, the romantic tension between Pam and Jim is palpable. We see Jim and Roy face off on the basketball court, competing for Pam's attention until Michael ends the game and declares his team the winner, citing a "flagrant personal, intentional foul."

Rumors of an office downsizing are rife among the employees in *The Alliance*. Dwight believes that foming a *Survivor*-style "alliance" with Jim will benefit him, which Jim plays along with. Pam and Jim spend the day teasing Dwight. At closing time, Jim grabs Pam's hand for a moment while they laugh about their day. At this moment, Roy appears and accuses Jim of hitting on his fiancée. When Jim explains that it was related to an office prank and goes to Dwight to back him up, Dwight feigns ignorance and Jim is left embarrassed.

The season ends with *Hot Girl*. Michael allows Katy, an attractive door-to-door handbag sales person, to spend the day in the office in the desperate hope that he can drive her home, only to have Jim step in at the last moment and offer her a lift, leaving a jealous Pam and Michael behind.

PROFILE
Steve Carell

Born August 16, 1962 in Massachusetts, Steve Carell wasn't always on a path to the stage. He completed a degree in history in Ohio, and then planned to move on to law school. However, during the process of applying he realized that law wasn't for him. Having dabbled in improvisation during his degree, Carell headed for Chicago to attend the legendary improv house *The Second City*. From here, he was able to get a few bit parts, but his first big break was on *The Dana Carvey Show*, where he was hired alongside fellow unknown, Stephen Colbert. Both Colbert and Carell would then go on to roles as correspondents on *The Daily Show*, Comedy Central's highly successful news and satire program.

When Carell auditioned for the role of Michael Scott in *The Office*, he had only watched half of the first episode of the UK series, having stopped when he became worried he would mimic Ricky Gervais' character David Brent. The producers saw something more than just an impersonation in Carell's performance and cast him in the role. After the first season of *The Office* got off to a shaky start in terms of ratings, Carell was cast in the film *The 40-Year-Old Virgin*, which proved he could carry the lead in movies too. As *The Office* became hugely successful, Carell would go on to star in the films *Little Miss Sunshine* (2006), *Dan in Real Life* (2007) and *Get Smart* (2008). He took on a more serious role, for which he was critically acclaimed, in *Foxcatcher* (2014), where he portrayed philanthropist and wrestling enthusiast John du Pont.

Carell and his wife, Nancy, (née Walls) live in Los Angeles and have two children, Elisabeth Anne (born May 2001) and John (born June 2004). Nancy can also been seen in *The Office* playing Carol Stills, the real estate agent who becomes Michael's love interest and rival to Jan. While Carell looks back fondly on *The Office*, he has stated publicly that he would not be part of a reboot of the show. Reflecting on the show, Carell says, "It was the most exciting time, and all of those people are my friends. We all love it. It was a special thing. It was a special thing before people thought it was a special thing. It was special to us, before other people started feeling that way."

JIM AND PAM'S GUIDE
to office romance

Your Account Stated to Date-If Error Is Found Return at Once.

How did you two meet and fall in love?

Jim: It was my first day at Dunder Mifflin. Pam took me aside and said, "Enjoy this moment, because you're never going back to this time before you met your desk-mate, Dwight."

Pam: When I met Jim at work, I was dating Roy from the warehouse. I saw Jim as a friend, someone I could talk to about stuff Roy didn't want to talk about. Like my feelings and my interests.

Michael: Boy did that one come from left field. I did NOT see that one. I thought Jim spent a bunch of time at the reception desk because he couldn't use the copier.

What did you do for your last wedding anniversary?

Jim: I arranged a babysitter so Pam and I could go to our favorite Italian restaurant.

Pam: There we were, enjoying our appetizers and a bottle of wine by candlelight. And Michael walks in.

Michael: I wanted to find a way to commemorate the occasion so I snuck everyone in from the office through the kitchen and, just as they were about to have a second glass of wine, we all streamed into the room, performing an *a cappella* version of "Forever" by Chris Brown, just like at their wedding. You should have seen their faces. They looked just as happy as when I did it on their wedding day.

When was the exact moment you both knew that the other person was the one for you?

Jim: From the first moment I spoke to her at the reception desk, I knew I wanted to spend the rest of my life with Pam.

Pam: Jim came up to me in the kitchen and said, "This might sound weird, and there's no reason for me to know this, but that mixed-berry yogurt you're about to eat has expired."

Michael: I first knew I loved Pam when I saw her walk into work in the cutest twin set and pearls. Wait, can you repeat the question?

After a promising first season and Steve Carell's newly found fame from his role in Judd Apatow's highly successful film *The 40-Year-Old Virgin*, NBC ordered a full 22-episode season. This season is bookended by *The Dundies* and *Casino Night*, arguably two of the most iconic episodes in the show's history. Both episodes take the team out of the office and into a party setting. *The Dundies* centers around Michael handing out embarrassing office awards and inflicting his own comedic and musical performances on the team at a local Chili's. Pam has too much to drink and enjoys a playful flirtation with Jim.

Romance-obsessed customer service officer Kelly Kapoor starts dating the new office "temp," Ryan Howard, the night before Valentine's Day, much to his dismay when he realizes the date. We also learn of the secret tryst between Dwight and office accountant Angela Martin, when the documentary camera finds them making love at Jim's barbecue in a backyard cubby house. Romance is also in the air in *The Client*, when Michael sleeps with his boss Jan Levinson-Gould after a successful margarita-fueled sales pitch to an important client. Jan wakes up the next day regretting the incident. However,

Michael is now smitten, repeatedly declaring his romantic intentions to her, all of which are rejected.

We also discover that Michael has written a screenplay, *Threat Level Midnight*, when Pam discovers a printed copy in the office. The team stay back late at work to perform a hilarious read-through of the script and it is revealed that the bumbling sidekick in the story is based on Dwight. In *Booze Cruise*, the branch enjoy a boat party on the lake and Jim brings Katy as his date. Roy gets drunk and decides on a whim to announce a date for his wedding to Pam, surprising her in front of her co-workers. Jim realizes his feelings for Pam are still strong and breaks up with Katy on the boat. He confesses his feelings to Michael who unsurprisingly had "no idea."

In the final moments of the season, we are left hanging when Jim declares his feelings for Pam in the parking lot during *Casino Night*. After she rebuffs him, Pam calls her mother from inside the empty office to tell her about what happened. Jim enters and they share a passionate kiss, leaving every die-hard Jim and Pam fan reeling over the season break.

QUIZ: WHAT'S YOUR MANAGEMENT STYLE?

1. It is a new employee's first day. What do you do as a manager to ensure they get off to a good start?

A. From the start I want them to know that I will be there for them, as their friend as well as their boss. Maybe I'll take them to lunch at the local Hooters, just to make them feel comfortable.

B. I simply respond to every one of their questions with another question of a more philosophical nature.

C. I will prove to them that it is a fun place to work. Let's get some vodka up in this cranberry, and one for my friend!

D. I give them a nickname immediately. People love that!

2. One of your employees tells you that they are currently going through a messy divorce. How do you support them when they are in need without jeopardizing productivity?

A. There is nothing that a night of amateur improv can't fix.

B. I lost my forties and my dream house to a woman. I would simply tell them we all die alone, therefore we are all better off alone.

C. That makes me uncomfortable. Can you please repeat the question while I run away?

D. I'd probably perform a song for them. Something uplifting and definitely *a cappella*.

3. What motivates you to be the best manager you can be?

A. Knowing that above all else, my team sees me as their friend and is always loyal to me. Always. Without exception

B. The same thing that motivates us all – sex.

C. Fear. The fear of failing. The fear of saying the wrong thing. Also mime. I love mime!

D. When I wake every day, no matter whether I am the branch manager of a paper company or a janitor, I know I am representing Cornell University.

4. Do you think that it is ever appropriate to enter into a romantic relationship with someone you work with?

A. Yes, providing at least one of the participants is willing.
B. "Romantic relationship." It's interesting that you use those words together, don't you think?
C. Oh God, I don't even know anymore. I've got three kids! Now I'm uncomfortable.
D. Only if you are sure that they are the only woman in the world for you, your true love. I have personally met two of my true loves in the Scranton office.

5. A member of your team complains that they are being bullied at work because of their race. How do you handle this?

A. Sounds like it's time for one of my famous diversity celebrations. One activity I like to do is celebrity heads ... but for race.
B. This question amuses me because I don't see race. In my eyes we are all the same. We are primates, with only our instincts and pheromones to move us forward on our paths.
C. In the Southwest we've got a saying ... uh ... "Can you repeat the question?"
D. Woo hoo hoo I am NOT touching that. Next question.

6. Describe the perfect manager.

A. He must be the world's best boss, and the world's best friend. He could even be a woman.
B. Someone who has lived so intensely that their brain literally couldn't hold the memories in.
C. Someone who can read their employees' minds or, failing that, can tell if an employee can read his mind.
D. Ivy League–educated.

7. What is your favorite office Christmas party theme?

A. I don't care, as long as Toby isn't there.
B. Ah, Christmas. The time for us to look into the expressionless eyes of the people we try to love, and mark the time that has passed into nothingness.
C. Desert Christmas. In the Southwest, we don't need snow to have fun!
D. Anything where I can play a musical instrument for my co-workers.

8. What is your favorite office Halloween party costume?

A. I choose whatever the funniest thing that happened that year is, and I go as that. No matter what the repercussions are.
B. I do not attend Halloween parties. But aren't we all wearing a mask of some kind every day of our lives?
C. Linda Ronstadt, the greatest Arizonian who ever lived.
D. That is such a hard question! But my all-time favorite was when I came dressed as a cat ... from Cats.

Mostly A's

YOU ARE → **MICHAEL SCOTT**

You are fundamentally a good person — however, your desire to be loved by your employees may distract you from your duties as manager. Take your own advice here: don't ever, for any reason, do anything, to anyone, for any reason, ever, no matter what, no matter where, or who, or who you are with, or where you are going, or where you've been, ever, for any reason whatsoever.

"YOU MISS 100% OF THE SHOTS YOU DON'T TAKE -WAYNE GRETZKY"
-MICHAEL SCOTT

Mostly B's

YOU ARE → **ROBERT CALIFORNIA**

You are a complex person who is most likely overqualified for the job you are doing now. Like the ancient primates you evolved from, you listen to your instincts. You can smell it all — fear, leadership and unfortunately the office men's room.

There is no such thing as a product. Don't ever think there is. There is only sex. Everything is sex.

Mostly C's

| YOU ARE | → | DEANGELO VICKERS |

Your management style might divide your employees. Especially if you pick your favorites and give them special treatment. Motivating your team is important. However, you may want to stay away from motivational juggling mime. They are simply not ready for it.

Mostly D's

YOU ARE → **ANDY BERNARD**

Your employees like you as a person — in fact sometimes they worry about you as a person. Try not to let your heart rule everything you do. And if you do want to express your heart, resist the urge to do it in song.

By its third season, *The Office* had won a Golden Globe for Best Television Series – Musical or Comedy. Steve Carell had also taken home a Golden Globe for Best Actor in the same category. In Scranton, time has also moved forward since we left the office on *Casino Night*. We are intrigued to discover that Roy and Pam never got married, as Pam backed out because of "cold feet." However, to our disappointment, Jim has transferred to the Stamford branch after Pam rejected him for a second time, off camera.

At the Stamford branch, Jim immediately hits it off with Karen Filippelli, one of the Stamford sales reps. They begin dating. When the Stamford branch is merged with Scranton, with Michael Scott at the helm, Karen moves down from Stamford. Pam is forced to watch Karen and Jim's romance blossom while she negotiates her new life as a single woman. We meet Andy Bernard from the Stamford branch, a driven but hopeless sales rep whose lack of self-awareness and need to be loved rivals Michael Scott himself. Phyllis marries her boyfriend, local refrigerator salesman Bob Vance.

In *Back from Vacation*, we find out that, despite her public rejection of Michael, Jan has spent her summer break with him at a *Sandals* resort in Jamaica. When Dunder Mifflin's head bully Todd Packer refuses to believe that the vacation happened, Michael emails him a revealing photograph of himself and Jan on the beach. Mayhem ensues in the warehouse when Michael accidentally emails the photo to "Packaging" instead of "Packer."

Jim and Karen both apply for the same job at Dunder Mifflin corporate in New York, and it looks like they might be about to make a significant move forward as a couple. Then, in a touching moment that was sure to be replayed over and over again by fans, Pam talks to the camera assuming that Jim has likely got the job in New York and is moving away. Unexpectedly, Jim bursts into the room and asks her on a date that evening. Pam, and millions of *Office* fans worldwide are overwhelmed with joy.

When you work in HR, everybody at one time or another will come to you with a problem – from resolving simple issues like people forgetting their social security number to explaining complex questions that Dwight has about the female anatomy.

Some of the employees at Dunder Mifflin need more attention than others. I probably spend most of my day processing HR complaints about Michael (from all around the office) and Jim (from Dwight only). I usually just throw the Jim complaints in the trash. But I actually have a whole shelf in the warehouse stacked with the complaints about Michael. It's so tall now I have to use a forklift to get stuff up there. Sometimes I just go out there to be alone. Sometimes I just stand looking at the boxes and I cry.

The Finer Things Club, which Oscar, Pam and I started, has really become the highlight of my life. I mean "week." Pam came up with the idea and I guess I just like making her happy. I'm really into reading books, fine films and culture, unlike Jim.

When you spend your whole day working with people and talking about their relationships, it can make coming home to an empty house at night feel pretty lonely. But there are things you can do to feel less alone. I leave the front door of my apartment open so I can hear the couple next door talking to each other. That's comforting. I also sleep with a pillow that I put some Victoria's Secret underwear on. That's comforting too.

I have six roommates, which are better than friends because they have to give you one month's notice before they leave.

CRUSHING YOUR ENEMIES

The ultimate survival guide from Dwight Schrute

In an ideal world, I would have all ten fingers on my left hand so my right hand could just be a fist for punching.

I see everyone in the office as a potential enemy. You can't trust anyone. Since I was a baby I have been in training. For what, you may ask? Simple. I am prepared for any kind of danger that may arise. Terrorism, wildfire. A sudden nuclear war. Someone super-gluing my office phone to the receiver.

In every aspect of my life, I keep a cache of items that I need to survive. In my car I keep a series of warm pelts, knives, spare gasoline, spare "spare" gasoline. I have enough deer jerky and fermented beet juice to use as rations for ten days. That should be long enough for me to find a fresh water supply and kill enough game to feed myself and Mose for a month. In my desk I keep a small kerosene-fueled generator which, if required, could power the office for up to three days. That means that even in the event of a full loss of electricity, Dunder Mifflin could go on selling paper. I also keep a parachute in case of fire. If a fire occurs, I would simply exit the second floor by breaking a window and floating safely down to my vehicle.

Before entering any building I like to first inspect it for booby traps that may have been set by my enemies. At work this is a relatively easy, 30- to 60-minute job. When visiting a new building, such as that of a client, it can take me upwards of two hours to ensure that I will not be subject to a trap – three hours if they have air-conditioner ducts that I can climb through.

When you meet an enemy, you must be willing to put in the effort it takes to destroy them. No matter how uncomfortable. Does it involve going without food or water for 12 hours while hiding behind drywall? You must do it. My motto is, "no retreat, no surrender." I learned this from a movie I saw once called *No Retreat, No Surrender*. I once stalked a man 50 miles into the forest in the snow after I caught him stealing beets from my farm. It turned out to be a dog.

What is the most romantic gift you have given your partner?

Pam: A night at Dwight's beet farm. He will certainly never forget that.

Jim: I gave her my parents' house in Scranton. Wait, is that romantic?

Phyllis: That's personal, but let's just say I installed a gym at my house. We call it "the bedroom."

Bob: I gave Phyllis a 40-gallon chest freezer. That thing could freeze a deer in about 15 minutes flat.

What are your partner's best qualities?

Pam: Well he did once break up my parents.

Jim: Did Pam really say that? I think Pam's best quality is that she forgave me for breaking up her parents.

Phyllis: Bob is reliable. He is cool. He never stops working. Kind of like a refrigerator.

Bob: Phyllis is a good woman. A strong woman. A kind woman. And she is a firecracker in the bedroom.

Describe your perfect date night.

Pam: Anything without the kids.

Jim: I'm going to agree with Pam here.

Phyllis: Dinner at my favorite restaurant and sneaking to the powder room after the entrée for a quick "dessert" with Bob.

Bob: I once took Phyllis to a refrigeration conference. And we did it in the back of a refrigerated truck.

What is your secret for making love last forever?

Pam: I don't need a secret, I know Jim will love me forever.

Jim: Sharing a common enemy: Dwight.

Phyllis: I keep the fire in my heart burning by listening to the *Fifty Shades of Grey* audiobook.

Bob: You've got to treat your woman right. Don't let them forget that you love 'em. And that you work just upstairs in their building. I'm talking flowers. Candy. Plush toys so big she has to carry them out like a firefighter.

UNT
WARD

r Is Found Return at Once.

SEASON 4 overview

Season 4 kicks off violently in *Fun Run* when Michael accidentally runs over purchasing assistant Meredith Palmer with his car in the office parking lot. While in hospital recovering from her injuries, it is discovered that Meredith also has rabies. Michael organizes a fun run in her honor to deflect his guilt, making the unwise decision to "carbo-load" for the race by eating fettuccine alfredo while running. Jan has lost her job at Dunder Mifflin corporate due to her unstable behavior and has moved into Michael's modest apartment in Scranton to work on her candle business, "Serenity by Jan."

When Ryan is promoted to Regional Manager after Jan's dismissal, he immediately breaks up with Kelly and moves to New York where he launches the website *Dunder Mifflin Infinity*. Dwight and Angela also break up in a dramatic fashion when Dwight kills her favorite cat, Sprinkles. Andy begins courting Angela, but struggles to get any more affection than the occasional neck nuzzling. We find out that, as we suspected, Jim and Karen have broken up on their trip to New York. However, Jim and Pam seem to still be "just friends." When the film crew catch Pam and Jim meeting secretly after work, they admit that they are dating, delighting fans across the universe.

Jim realizes that Dwight and Angela have been seeing each other and is excited to tell Pam, but she already knows about it. In an effort to win back Angela's affections, Dwight brings a stray cat named Garbage into the office as a gift for Angela. Kelly tries to win back Ryan by telling him she is pregnant, on one of his office visits. When Ryan realizes that Kelly has lied to him, he plucks up the courage to ask Pam out on a date. He is left feeling sorry for himself when she tells him that Jim is her boyfriend.

In the final episode, *Goodbye, Toby*, we learn that Jim is planning to propose to Pam and has splashed out on fireworks for the occasion. However, his plans are foiled when Andy proposes to Angela at the party and she accepts.

CREED THOUGHTS!

Hey-o, everyone out there in SyberWorld.

Creed Bratton coming at you, here from my perch as Quality Assurance Manager at Dunder Mifflin. Ryan helped me set up this blog so I could share observations on the world around me. He told me it would get on the internet if I type it into this document. Or maybe it was the World Wide Web. I don't really know the difference. What I do know is that I don't like that Ryan kid much. I don't trust the young. Too much hair product. Not enough shaving product. They other day I was late for a meeting and Ryan asked me why I didn't send him a text message to tell him I was running late. What the hell is a text message? You know who else I don't trust? That chick Michael hit with a car. I think she's a plant from corporate. I know when I'm being watched. How come? Because I'm a wanted felon in several states.

Me, I'm used to living on the fringes. You know the only difference between me and a homeless man is this job. I will do whatever it takes to survive ... like I did when I was a homeless man. Before that I used to be in a band. In the sixties. That was a time. I stole military-grade LSD from the army when I was working in the New England Coast Guard. I hid it in my sack and snuck it across the state line. To Woodstock. I don't remember Woodstock much. But one thing I do remember is the women. I don't recall individuals, it was more like a sea of them. And no amount of coast guard training can prepare you for that. Someone stole my stash on the bus back to San Fran. I tried telling the police but they just wanted to arrest me. I told them I had to go the bathroom and climbed out the window. After that I had to lie low for a while. Sit it out. I was on the run for about 20 years.

Wait. Dwight just said something to the tall guy (Rob???). Apparently he sold a pallet of the wrong copy paper. We sell copy paper here? This is news to me. I thought this was a dog food company.

I've been involved in a number of cults, both as a leader and a follower. You have more fun as a follower, but you make more money as a leader.

DRESSING FOR SUCCESS

with Andy Bernard

As the only Ivy League–educated employee at Dunder Mifflin, the burden is on me to represent my alma mater by always dressing for success. Some people say that the preppy look went out ten years ago. To those people I say, "You are a loser and I hate you." I like to follow a simple rule for dressing myself. I abide by the Three C's: Clean, Collegiate and Cornell. Gabe told me I dress like my life is one long brunch. Michael said my clothes remind him of Easter, which I take as a compliment.

On the bottom

Denim? No thank you sir! Chinos only for me. I like to get them in my trouser press and really steam those seams until you could cut butter with 'em. As for shoes, I want to see my reflection in them. And nobody sees my toesies but me. I don't even wear flip flops on the family yacht.

On top

T-shirts? I've never worn one. I'll take a crisp, ironed shirt with a bow tie and some knitwear, a-thank-you-very-much. Knitwear is so versatile. I prefer a pastel knit. In winter, knitwear keeps you warm. In summer, all you have to do is sling it over your polo and you've got yourself some shade right there. I have the same polo shirt in eight different colors. And I'm not afraid to wear 'em close to the old skin. Tight enough to see a nipple or two. Elbow patches on Jacket? Yes please. Don't forget that the ladies go crazy for a pinstripe or a candy stripe.

Hair and accessories

As for the old mop top, you can't go wrong with a sensible side part. Comb that sucker down with some pomade. When I really want to impress, I make sure I add some flair to my outfit by including some Cornell branding. Maybe a cap or a commemorative stick pin. To me, the best accessory to any outfit is a smile. And maybe a song.

LEAF
LEAF
LEAF
LEAF
LEAF
LEAF
PRO

TOT
CAS
CHA

SI

KELLY AND RYAN'S
guide to dating

KELLY'S ADVICE

Having a boyfriend is the most important thing in the world. If you don't have a hot guy who loves you, what is the point? If you want to attract a guy, you have to dress nice. Looking good is so important. I shop online, not at the mall like Pam. I look really good in white. So whenever I want to impress a guy, I wear a white dress. Even to weddings.

Guys are always intimidated by me. That's why I always make the first move. I guess you could say I'm half diet bitch, half fitness bitch and half business bitch. If you want to keep a guy, you have to make him jealous. If a bit of healthy jealousy doesn't work, you have to take action. Tell him that you are pregnant with his baby. Tell

him you are pregnant with his father's baby. Once a man has terror like that in his heart, he'll do anything you say.

If a guy doesn't want to be with me, I am adult enough to handle it. Like, whatever. I just pray they never ever find someone else ever and also that they die of unhappiness.

Who says exactly what they're thinking? What kind of game is that?

RYAN'S ADVICE

If you want to sleep with someone you work with, you'll probably need to start dating them. The key to this is dating while avoiding commitment. This is how I do it. Once things start getting serious, I tell them I'm moving to another city for work. Or traveling in a country that they really don't want to visit. Kelly is different. Kelly scares me. She once chased me across the state line in her car when I didn't respond to one of her texts. I didn't know I had to respond – it was just a string of emojis and a question mark.

When I was Vice President, North East Region and Director of New Media at Dunder Mifflin, I used to meet lots of women. With a title like that on your business card, you can pretty much take home any woman in New York. I mean maybe not Manhattan but Brooklyn for sure. Okay, Staten Island. When you look the way I do, it's not just women who give you attention. Sometimes I catch Michael staring at me through the blinds in his office and it terrifies me.

I'd rather she be alone than with somebody. Is that love?

SEASON 5
overview

The season opens with Pam finally following her dream of attending art school in New York, but the distance begins to place a strain on her relationship with Jim. This culminates in a romantic reunion at a gas station on a rainy afternoon halfway between Scranton and New York, where Jim proposes. So many years of loving each other from afar are vindicated when Pam says yes. In this season we meet the sweet and awkward HR representative Holly Flax, when she replaces Toby. Naturally, Michael immediately falls for her and an awkward courtship begins.

It turns out that Angela has been secretly seeing Dwight behind Andy's back, when Phyllis exposes the truth in *Moroccan Christmas*. This results in an office "duel" between Dwight and Andy, which ends with them both breaking up with Angela. In *New Boss*, Charles Miner is introduced as the new regional manager who will be replacing Ryan. The women in the office swoon and Jim finds it difficult to give a good first impression of himself to the new boss.

Unhappy after fifteen years of loyal service, Michael Scott leaves Dunder Mifflin to form The Michael Scott Paper Company, taking Ryan and Pam with him. Pam is left with the unenviable task of preventing Michael from procrastinating his days away, which proves to be a challenge. The team end up bickering in a tiny makeshift "office" in the Dunder Mifflin building with leaking pipes and the sound of flushing toilets throughout the day. Eventually David Wallace tries to buy the company for $60,000. Michael makes the demand that he gets his old job back alongside Ryan and Pam as salespeople.

We are also introduced to sweet receptionist Erin Hannon, who replaces Pam when she defects with Michael. Erin's naivety shines through when we find out that she has a crush on Andy, who she describes as the "coolest guy in the office." Holly and Michael are reunited temporarily at the end of the season in *Company Picnic,* when they put on an HR skit together. Despite Holly arriving with her new boyfriend, AJ, in tow, Michael tells her that he believes they will one day get back together, which he is fine with because he is "in no rush." Pam hurts her ankle in the volleyball tournament and we are overjoyed to discover, while she is in the hospital for an x-ray, that she is pregnant.

DWIGHT AND ANGELA'S LOVE TIMELINE

2005

Dwight and Angela have already begun a secret romance. However, we only find out when the documentary cameras spot them making love in the backyard at Jim's barbecue.

2006

The couple continues to see each other secretly. However, Dwight almost exposes their relationship in *Casino Night* when he kisses her on the cheek after winning at craps.

2007

Angela tasks Dwight with feeding her sick cat Sprinkles while she is visiting Meredith in hospital. Dwight finds the cat to be very ill and decides to euthanize Sprinkles as a "mercy killing." Angela is devastated and they break up. Enter Andy Bernard, who begins to court Angela. However, it is clear from the start that their relationship is a farce, as she keeps Andy at a distance most of the time.

2008

Andy proposes to Angela at Toby's farewell party. She says yes. However, we find out that she has already begun cheating on Andy with Dwight, often sneaking to an office store room to make love. Andy and Angela decide to get married at Schrute Farms, based on Angela's insistence that she is married on hand-plowed land. During a rehearsal of the ceremony, Dwight steps into the groom position and it is clear that he has brought in a real priest to marry him and Angela.

At the Christmas party that year, Phyllis reveals to everyone in the office, except for Andy, that Angela is cheating with Dwight.

2009

Michael Scott is the person who finally breaks the news of Angela's cheating to Andy, before immediately escaping the office to have a meeting with David Wallace. Andy challenges Dwight to a duel, for which Angela is the prize. When it is revealed during the duel that Andy and Angela have had sex during their relationship, Dwight ends the duel and spurns Angela. Andy also admits defeat and she is left with no boyfriend at all.

2010

It is revealed that Dwight and Angela once signed a baby contract, with many convoluted stipulations. When Dwight tries to dispute the contract, the two agree to have sex five times at Angela's request.

2011

Angela begins dating Senator Robert Lipton and falls pregnant.

2012

Angela gives birth to baby Philip. Dwight suspects that he is the father and asks Angela to get a paternity test. Angela tells Dwight that Robert is Philip's father.

2013

Angela finds out that Robert has been having an extra-marital affair with Oscar. They remain together for a few months, but they break up when Robert comes out as being gay in a press conference. Angela admits that she still loves Dwight, however he is dating another woman, Jessica. Jim convinces Dwight that Angela is the right woman for him and he decides to chase her in his car and propose to her on the side of the road.

2014

Angela and Dwight get married at Schrute Farms.

Angela on Dwight: "Dwight has been practicing karate for years. When we were dating, I would help him with his strength training. He would strap me to his chest in a BabyBjörn made for fat children and do lunges across the farm."

Dwight to Angela: "I will raise 100 of your children with 100 of your lovers if it means I can be with you."

THE MANY LOVE INTERESTS
of Michael Scott

Jan Levinson

What worked: Their sexual chemistry. Despite being initially repulsed by his personality, Jan was unable to resist sleeping with Michael when they got drunk together for the first time. In the *Dinner Party* episode, it was revealed that they keep a video camera on a tripod at the end of their bed.

What didn't work: After being Michael's manager for so long, Jan was never able to respect him. She also drank heavily and, even though she wanted to have children, she didn't want them with him.

Carol Stills

What worked: Carol thought Michael was kind and sweet when they bumped into each other at the ice rink and he got along with her children.

What didn't work: Michael was too keen and scared Carol off. In *Diwali*, he not only proposed to her but also produced a photo where he had digitally inserted himself amongst her family.

Helene Beesly

What worked: Michael was Helene's post-marriage rebound guy, but she really liked him as a person.

What didn't work: Even though Pam was not happy about Michael dating her mom at first, she came around to the idea and they went on a double date with her and Jim. When Helene revealed her age to Michael, he broke up with her immediately at the table.

```
O • C

139 • +
 20 • =
159 • *
```

Reg. No.	Clerk	ACCOUNT FORWARD		
1				
2				
3				
4				
5				
6				
7				
8				
9				
10				
11				
12				
13				
14				
15				

Your Account Stated to Date-If Error Is Found Return at Once.

0•c
64•+
9•=
3•*

Donna Newton

What worked: Sparks flew initially when Donna almost threw Michael out of her bar, Sid & Dexter, during happy hour. She visited him at the office under the guise of ordering paper and their mutual attraction was clear.

What didn't work: It turned out that Donna was married, and that she was cheating on her husband with Michael.

Holly Flax

Why they worked: In many ways, Holly is Michael in a woman's body. She is sweet but gullible, and they have a similar sense of humor. Holly often drops bad impersonations into conversations at work, much to the confusion of everyone in the office but Michael, who adores her. Holly and Michael are proof that there is someone special for everyone.

0•c
139•+
20•=
159•*

0•c
119•+
45•=
164•*

Do I need to be liked? Absolutely not. I like to be liked. I enjoy being liked. I have to be liked, but it's not like this compulsive need to be liked, like my need to be praised.

The history of
DUNDER MIFFLIN

Dunder Mifflin was founded in 1949 by Robert Dunder and Robert Mifflin. The two Roberts met on a tour of Dartmouth University and ended up drinking together at a local alehouse. In this alehouse, they came up with an idea for a business, which they both quit Dartmouth to pursue. The business would be called Dunder Mifflin and they would supply metal brackets for construction. The first warehouse was founded in New York then, in order to take advantage of significantly lower property prices, they branched out to Scranton, Stamford, Utica, Camden, Buffalo and Yonkers.

In the early 1950s, Dunder Mifflin decided to move from brackets to distributing cabbage, mostly grown in crops in Texas. Rumor has it that Dunder was descended from the Pennsylvania Dutch and, as a result, had an unhealthy mistrust of modern construction practices. When a drought wiped out almost all of the cabbage crops in Texas in the late 1950s, Mifflin had the idea that selling paper may be a more viable option.

It is said in business circles that Robert Dunder was difficult to work with. This may have contributed to Robert Mifflin killing himself in 1972. There are industry rumors of a suicide note being found by Mifflin's body reading, "Dunder, I hate everything you choose to be." However, at the time of this book's printing, there has been no convincing evidence of this.

Dunder Mifflin focussed on paper for the next five decades, refusing to diversify their business despite the rapid decline in paper use brought on by the computing revolution. Dunder himself met with some of the pioneers of Silicon Valley and was given the opportunity to purchase a large amount of IBM stock before the personal computer boom. Dunder declined the offer and famously refused to use a computer in his office until his retirement in 1985. Robert Dunder retired to a modest lifestyle, living in a home for the elderly in Dupont, Pennsylvania.

Some other notable dates in Dunder Mifflin History

1985: Ed Truck is promoted to regional manager of Dunder Mifflin Scranton

1992: Michael Scott is hired as a salesman

1996: Michael wins Salesman of the Year

2001: Ed Truck retires and Michael Scott is made Regional Manager of Dunder Mifflin Scranton

2002: Michael attends the Halloween party dressed as Monica Lewinsky

2003: Michael attends the Halloween party dressed as Monica Lewinsky, again

2004: Michael attends the Halloween party dressed as Janet Jackson's boob

2005: The PBS documentary crew arrives to commence shooting *The Office: An American Workplace*

0188451

Date _____ 20 ____

Clerk | ACCOUNT FORWARD

SCOTT'S TOTS

The most awkward episode of a sitcom ever?

The *Scott's Tots* episode of Season 6 has been widely regarded by fans as almost impossible to watch due to its extremely cringeworthy storyline. There is no doubt that *The Office* is one of the all-time greatest binge-watch comedies, with fans claiming that as soon as they watch it all the way through, they will simply start back at the first episode and go around again. However, it seems that many fans deliberately skip over *Scott's Tots* because some of the scenes are simply too painful to watch.

The episode opens with receptionist Erin discussing Michael's daily itinerary with Pam. Pam is surprised to read that the "Michael Scott Foundation" is still in existence, something that *Office* fans were at that time blissfully yet to learn about. We learn that Michael has been putting off meeting with some students he made a huge promise to ten years earlier. Michael promised them that if they graduated from high school he would pay for their college tuition. Pam and Erin are shocked by the revelation. As Michael himself puts it, "I have made some empty promises in my life but hands down that was the most generous."

Michael is hesitant to face the kids but Pam forces him, sending Erin along for moral support. His guilt intensifies as he enters the aptly named "The Michael Gary Scott Reading Room" to a round of applause and cheers from a class full of students wearing T-shirts emblazoned with "Scott's Tots." The group immediately erupts into a choreographed singing and dancing performance, shouting in unison "Hey Mr Scott, what chu gonna do? What chu gonna do? Make our dreams come true!"

Michael becomes increasingly nervous during this spectacle and is eventually moved to tears when a male student speaks of how Michael's promise has inspired him to become the next President Obama. When it's Michael's turn to take the podium, *Office* viewers hold their collective breath as Michael announces, "I am never going to forget today ... I have done something stupid which I would like to share." After stalling for a few minutes, Michael admits the truth. He tells the kids that he will not be able to pay for anybody's tuition. The class erupts in anger and dismay.

He tells them, "Now, I can't pay for your college. But you don't have to go to class to be in class. Online classes are a viable option to a traditional college experience. And the best way to access those courses is with your own personal laptop. Which is rendered useless,

without batteries. And I have one for each of you." Michael has offered the students laptop batteries instead of paid college tuition. The booing and protests continue.

When leaving the school, a male student takes Michael aside, to confront him one-on-one and eventually convinces him to write four checks for $1000 each, to pay for his school books for college. As they drive back to the office, Michael is shell-shocked by the experience. Erin hums the Scott's Tots song while Michael bemoans, "I destroyed fifteen young lives today." Erin replies: "The principal told me that ninety percent of Scott's Tots are on track to graduate and that's thirty-five percent higher than the rest of the school."

Only Michael Scott could return from a day like this believing he had done the right thing. He and Erin both hum the tune in unison as they drive back to the office. Finally our pain is over as the episode comes to an end. For further support, you can visit a Subreddit called r/*CannotWatchScottsTots* with over 13,000 subscribers. Those of us left permanently scarred by *Scott's Tots* are not alone.

ASK ACCOUNTS

ANGELA

OSCAR

KEVIN

Dear Accounts,

I come from a religious background and planned
to remain a virgin until my wedding night.
However, lately my boyfriend has been asking me to
"go all the way" and I am finding it hard to say no.
Should I give in to my feelings of lust?

Frustrated in Nashville

Kevin: Oh yeah. You should totally give in to your feelings of lust.

Angela: Under no circumstances should you give in to these urges, unless you want to look like a cheap harlot. There are some alternatives that I find leave your partner satisfied without the sin, fuss and mess involved in sexual activity. My suggestion: neck nuzzling. When I was with Andy, I would allow him to nuzzle my neck for up to ten minutes at a time. If a man asks for anything more than that in the first year, he is disgusting.

Dear Accounts,

I am gay and feel that it is time to let people at my work know. However, my boss can be a bit of a joker and I fear that he will make a fool out of me. Should I talk to him first or simply announce it to the office?

John, Chicago

Oscar: When I was outed in the office by Michael, he subjected the entire staff to a seminar on homosexuality that was mortifying for me. To make it even worse, he kissed me in front of the office to prove he wasn't homophobic. If you want my advice, keep it to yourself for as long as humanly possible. Although, in my case I got three months' paid holiday and a car out of it.

Angela: Why do you have to come out at all? If you pray hard enough, you can change anything about yourself.

Dear Accounts,

I am getting married this fall and my bridesmaids want to choose their own dresses, including the color. I want to tell them that it's my special day and my choice, but I also don't want them to hate me. What should I do?

Carol, Santa Barbara

Angela: There should be no choice at all, for you or for the members of your party. Brides wear white and bridesmaids wear off-white or cream. Any other color is whorish.

Kevin: Remember when Angela got married to that senator? If Angela can get a gay man to marry her, maybe I could get a lesbian to marry me. That's hot.

PROFILE
Jenna Fischer

Jenna Fischer was born Regina Marie Fischer on March 7, 1974 and grew up in Missouri. Fischer attended Truman State University where she earned a Bachelor of Arts in theater with a minor in journalism. Somewhat fortuitously, Fischer worked as a receptionist for a time after she graduated. In 2004, she directed and starred in a mockumentary called *LolliLove* alongside her husband James Gunn. She earned the Screen Actors Guild Emerging Actor award for her performance. However, it would be three years before her next significant acting role, after successfully auditioning for the role of Pam Beesly in *The Office*.

"I studied theater in college, and I really wanted to be an actress and play a lot of different roles," said Fischer. "Then I made landing on a television comedy my main focus." Audiences immediately fell in love with Pam and Jim. On her acting partner John Krasinski, Fischer was famously quoted as saying, "John and I have real chemistry ... There's like a real part of me that is Pam and a real part of him that's Jim. And those parts of us were genuinely in love with one another." However, Krasinski has said that he thought that was "wildly misquoted ... as far as how she was quoted about saying we were 'genuinely in love,' I think that was taken wildly out of context and I feel bad for her." Fischer even kept the prop engagement ring that Jim gave Pam on the show.

In 2007 she received a Primetime Emmy nomination for Outstanding Supporting Actress in a Comedy Series and had major roles in the highly successful comedy films *Blades of Glory* and *Walk Hard: The Dewey Cox Story*. Fischer divorced James Gunn in 2008 and married screenwriter Lee Kirk in 2010. They had their first child, a son, in 2011, for which the pregnancy was written into *The Office*'s eighth season. Fischer gave birth to their second child, a daughter, in 2014.

Return at Once.

MEREDITH'S FAVORITE cocktail recipes

Hangover Cocktail

Everybody gets hangovers at work sometimes. I have them almost every day. A lot of people say you've just gotta get back on the horse and take some hair of the dog. And I'm no princess when it comes to doing just that. If I knock back one of these babies before 10 am I am good to go again by lunchtime.

Ingredients

2 crushed-up cold and flu tablets – the ones you get from behind the counter

1 shot of vodka – this is not negotiable

1 tablespoon of instant coffee powder

seltzer to top it up

Method

I like to mix this drink up and pour it into a large soda cup for consuming discreetly at my desk. You got a real bad hangover? I suggest taking one of these suckers into the shower to start your day.

You're welcome.

The Scranton Sampler

"Monongahela" is a rye whiskey distilled in southwestern Pennsylvania. Now I can't even pronounce it, let alone afford to buy the stuff from some kid with a beard and a bad attitude at one of the local distilleries. All I know is I like rye whiskey. I usually just grab a couple bottles of the cheap stuff from the supermarket on my lunch break. I don't mind having a few samples in the afternoon to help make the day go faster if you know what I mean. I pretty much take whatever is left after I drive home and shake up a few of these bad boys. I call this cocktail the Scranton Sampler because it's got sour cherries in it, which are grown out here in Pennsylvania. But like I said, local produce ain't cheap so I usually swap the fresh stuff for canned cherries. Anything soaked in high-fructose corn syrup helps sober me up after a long day in the office.

Ingredients

4–6 fresh Pennsylvanian sour cherries, pitted

half a lime (just the juice)

a splash of orange bitters

2 tablespoons of honey

3 ounces of whiskey (don't skimp on this)

fresh mint and cherries for garnish

Method

You've gotta mash the cherries up in a cocktail shaker along with the lime juice, bitters and honey.

Then you add your generous pour of whiskey and shake it all up.

Strain (or not, whatever – I don't have time to strain it – plus the cherries are a good meal replacement when you don't feel like cooking) into a glass filled with ice.

Garnish with mint and more cherries. And there you have it. A real meal in a glass.

I've had two men fight over me before. Usually it's over which one gets to hold the camcorder.

PROFILE
John Krasinski

John Krasinski was born on October 20, 1979 in Boston, Massachusetts. He attended Brown University, studied theater arts and graduated with an honors thesis as a playwright. He received training at the National Theater Institute in Connecticut and the Royal Shakespeare Company in the United Kingdom, then moved to New York City to pursue his dream of acting in film and television. In NYC he gained some small roles in TV shows and commercials. In 2000 he worked as an intern scriptwriter on the show *Late Night with Conan O'Brien*.

When he landed his role of Jim Halpert in *The Office*, Krasinski traveled to Scranton on a research trip, shooting some of the footage used in the opening credits on his own camera. He also interviewed real employees at paper companies. Audiences rooted for Jim Halpert from the start, sympathizing with his sense of humor and seemingly unrequited love for Pam Beesly, the receptionist. For his role as Jim he took home a Screen Actors Guild Award for Outstanding Performance by an Ensemble in a Comedy Series in 2007 and 2008. He has enjoyed a very successful acting career outside of *The Office*, starring in sports comedy *Leatherheads* (2008) and romantic comedy *Something Borrowed* (2011). Krasinski has gone through a dramatic physical transformation over the years, dieting and training intensely for his roles in *13 Hours* (2016) and TV series *Jack Ryan* (2018).

Krasinski met actress Emily Blunt in 2008 and they married in 2010. They have two children, Hazel (born in 2014) and Violet (born in 2016). In 2018 he wrote, directed and starred in the apocalyptic horror film *A Quiet Place* alongside Blunt, which received critical acclaim. Despite his success beyond *The Office,* Krasinski is appreciative of his time on the show, saying, "When people ask if I'm going to be sad that *The Office* is over, they don't even understand the depth of that question for me. It's an era of my life. No one would have known my name if it wasn't for the show."

In *The Meeting*, David gets together with Jim at corporate to discuss his future. Michael eavesdrops by hiding inside a cheese cart. When Jim misses out on the promotion, he tells Michael that he suspects him of talking David out of it. When Michael tries to apologize, David calls Michael back and proposes that Michael and Jim be co-managers of Scranton, with Michael handling clients and Jim handling day-to-day operations. This news crushes Dwight.

Pam and Jim decide to get married at Niagara Falls rather than Scranton, in an attempt to dissuade the team from coming. However, Michael announces an office shut-down for the Friday and Monday, and naturally the whole gang is in attendance. Michael's fixation on performing an all-team dance routine based on a viral YouTube video threatens to overshadow the day. However, in classic Jim and Pam fashion, they manage to steal a moment away for romance as they are married a second time by the boat captain with the waterfalls as a backdrop. We also witness the birth of Jim and Pam's first child, Cecelia, in this season.

In *Sabre*, a Florida-based printer sales company takes over Dunder Mifflin. We meet Sabre's CEO Jo Bennett, a straight-talking Southern businesswoman who doesn't take any flack. Jo's meek and insecure right-hand man, Gabe, is instantly unpopular with the team. Jo soon comes to the conclusion that Dunder Mifflin is the most grossly mismanaged company that she has ever seen. Michael is unhappy working under Jo and the Sabre regime, and turns to David Wallace for advice. He goes to his house and finds David worse for wear, depressed and disheveled in his new-found unemployment.

In *Whistleblower*, we find out that someone from inside the company has leaked to the media that Sabre's printers have a tendency to catch fire. Gabe goes on the warpath to find the culprit, but it turns out that almost everyone has leaked information to the outside world in some way. Michael is ambushed by a news crew and offers a public apology, which impresses Jo and she offers to help him out. Michael asks Jo to bring Holly back to the office and Jo says that she will see what she can do.

THE BEST of the guests

Kathy Bates as "Jo Bennett"

When Jo Bennett, CEO of Sabre, enters *The Office*, people sit up and listen. Jo is from the South, works hard and knows how to do business. Jo is tough. She collects guns, has survived breast cancer, can fly a plane and has slept with three of the same men as Truman Capote.

Best line: "You don't get to be the most powerful woman in Tallahassee by slacking off. You get there by working hard or marrying rich, and I did both."

Rob Riggle as "Captain Jack"

In *Booze Cruise* we meet Captain Jack, the handsome and charming ex navy officer who served in the Gulf War. During the cruise, Michael continually tries to assert control over him, however Captain Jack is extremely popular with the guests. He organizes a limbo contest and has a brief sexual encounter on the boat with Meredith. He also inspires Roy to set a date for his wedding to Pam.

Best line: [while seducing Meredith] "This is where Captain Jack drives the boat."

Jack Black as "Sam"

In *Stress Relief*, Jim and Pam illegally download the movie *Mrs Albert Hannaday* and are seen watching it in the break room several times throughout the episode. Jack Black plays Sam, a young man who starts a steamy affair with a significantly older woman, played by Cloris Leachman.

Best line: "Lilly stop! I don't care how much time we have left. I don't care what my friends say. And I don't care what your mom thinks! Frankly I'm pretty sure she's not making any sense! Please, move back to my apartment."

Will Ferrell as "Deangelo Vickers"

Deangelo Vickers is the first regional manager to step into Michael's shoes when he leaves and one of the most socially awkward and insecure characters we meet in the show. He tries to win the office over by performing a mimed juggling act, which leaves them all perplexed, and is so nervous he is unable to complete his duties as host of The Dundies.

Best line: "No matter how many times I reach out to Dwight, he doesn't seem to want anything to do with me. It reminds me of my relationship with my son. Except there, I'm the Dwight."

Ricky Gervais as "David Brent"

We finally see Michael Scott and his British counterpart, David Brent, meet in *The Seminar*. Their paths cross by an elevator, and they each make several jokes in poor taste. They leave with David asking Michael if there are any jobs available at Dunder Mifflin.

Best line: "Comedy is a place where the mind goes to tickle itself. That's what she said."

Tim Meadows as "Christian"

In *The Client*, Michael and Jan are to meet Christian, an important client, in order to convince him not to go to their competitor, Staples. At the last minute, Michael changes the venue from The Radisson to a Chili's, where he ends up bonding with Christian over baby back ribs and many margaritas.

Best line: "You were really brave. I mean, you put your arms out there, you slit your wrists. You said, 'World, this is my blood, it's red, just like yours. So love me.'"

Amy Adams as "Katy"

We first meet Katy in *Hot Girl*, when Michael allows her to sell purses from the conference room, hoping to get to know her better. She ends up getting a lift home with Jim and they start dating. However, Jim realizes that they have nothing in common during *Booze Cruise* and breaks up with her in a callous way.

Best line: "Goodnight! It was nice to meet some of you."

Idris Elba as "Charles Miner"

Charles Miner starts at Dunder Mifflin as the company vice president and Michael is put out by his lack of humor and matter-of-fact demeanor. His good looks attract the attention of many in the office. When he cancels Michael's "15 year anniversary" party, this is the final straw and Michael resigns.

Best line: "I am aware of the effect I have on women."

Ken Jeong as "Bill"

Michael attends an improv class and ruins every scene by taking out a gun and killing all the other improvisers, including Bill. When the teacher bans him from mentioning the gun, Michael whispers in Bill's ear, resulting in Bill placing his hands up in surrender.

Best line: "He told me he couldn't show it to me, but he has a gun."

Larry Wilmore as "Mr Brown"

We meet Mr Brown in *Diversity Day*. He has been sent from corporate to educate the office about diversity, after Michael's Chris Rock impersonation results in many complaints.

Best line: "Michael, I would love to have your permission to run this session. Can I have your permission?"

Wendi McLendon-Covey as "Concierge Marie"

When Michael and Oscar are sent to Winnipeg for work, Michael is excited to find there is a concierge at their hotel. He describes the role of concierge as the "Winnipeg equivalent of a geisha" and, after bumping into each other at a bar, Michael spends the night with her.

Best line: [Michael] "A concierge is like the Winnipeg equivalent of a geisha. This is a woman who has been trained in the fine art of fanciness and pleasure. And when you meet one, it is intoxicating. Just what the doctor ordered."

make friends first,
make sales second,
make love third.
In no particular order.

PROFILE
Rainn Wilson

Rainn Wilson was born on January 20, 1966 in Seattle. He attended the University of Washington where he began acting in local productions. Wilson was the most experienced of the main cast before he started in *The Office*, having made his film debut in *Galaxy Quest* (1999), *Almost Famous* (2000) and *Full Frontal* (2002). He also played Arthur Martin in the acclaimed HBO series *Six Feet Under* from 2003 to 2005.

Wilson initially auditioned for the role of Michael Scott in *The Office*, but it did not go well. Wilson himself describes the audition as him doing a "bad Ricky Gervais impression." It's hard to imagine anyone else playing Dwight Schrute, and his performance was recognized when he earned three consecutive Emmy nominations for Outstanding Supporting Actor in a Comedy Series. Of the show, Wilson has stated "the great thing about The Office and it being single-camera and the documentary style is that it's mostly a comedy, but 10 percent of it is we get to show the existential angst that exists in the American workplace."

Playing Dwight Schrute wasn't always easy for Wilson. He once said "the great challenge working on this show for me is wearing polyester all day long and having the worst haircut known to man at the top of my head and sitting under fluorescent lights. That is America, people. Polyester, bad haircuts, under fluorescent lights."

After meeting in an acting class at university, Wilson married Holiday Reinhorn in 1995. They have one son who was born in 2004. In addition to his acting work, Wilson published an autobiography called *The Bassoon King* in 2015 and co-founded the digital media company SoulPancake in 2008.

eturn at Once.

Famous Schrute Farm beet soup

This soup recipe has been handed down and enjoyed by the Schrute family since 1778. It is enjoyed 365 days a year as an evening staple at Schrute Farm. A variant of Schrute beet soup is served at family weddings, where the soup is served to the bride and groom in a hollowed-out gourd and then placed in the couple's shared matrimonial grave.

Cooking time: 12–13 hours

Ingredients

- 20 large Schrute Farm beets, unwashed. You may think you can substitute these for store-bought beets. WRONG. Only Schrute Farm beets have the flavor and soil content required for this soup.

- 100 cups of unfiltered Schrute Farm water, pumped from the natural springs by the historical outhouse at Schrute Farm. If this is not available, soak 5 Schrute beets and a shovelful of Pennsylvanian top soil in 100 cups of tap water in a children's-size bath over a long weekend or religious festival.

- 60 potatoes, unwashed and unpeeled

- 30 white turnips, unwashed with stems attached

- 5 large cabbages. Not red or purple. Nothing that you can buy at Whole Foods. FIVE LARGE WHITE CABBAGES purchased from a roadside cart or grown on your own family farm.

- 10 large yellow onions. You may wish to remove the skin. WRONG. The skin should remain on the onions.

- 40 tablespoons lard. We make our own lard at Schrute Farm out of rendered fat from the boiled carcasses of the Pennsylvanian barn shrew. This is the most sought-after shrew in the district due to the meat's distinct soil-like flavor, hence its status on Pennsylvania's endangered species list.

- 160 ounces unripe tomatoes, whole

- 40 cups beet broth. You can use the beet broth you will yield at the start of the cooking process below. Top up with extra outhouse spring water, 5 beets and a handful of unwashed corn husks.

- Additional beets to taste

Method

This soup should be cooked in a sterilized 50-gallon copper cauldron or, failing that, an empty family bathtub will suffice.

Place beets whole in the pot with water. Cook for 5–6 hours over high heat, or until beets are a brownish-gray color and have the aroma of damp soil.

While beets are cooking, prepare other vegetables. The potatoes, onions and turnips go in WHOLE. You may slice the cabbages into quarters for a less chunky soup.

When beets are gray and sponge-like to the touch, remove from pan.

Keep broth from the beets. This can be used later in your beet broth.

Add potatoes (whole) to the beet water, and cook over high heat for 2 hours.

Pour the shrew lard into a large skillet. Add whole onions and turnips. Sauté until blackened.

Add cabbage to skillet with onions and turnips, and cook over high heat until cabbage turns gray and sweats profusely.

Add cabbage, turnips, onions and beets to pot with potatoes.

Add whole unripe tomatoes and remaining beet broth. Do NOT stir.

Cook over high heat for 3–4 hours.

Serve COLD. Garnish with the sour milk of the family cow. You may think this soup requires seasoning with salt and pepper. WRONG. The natural flavor of the Schrute beets will suffice.

Sometimes I'll start a sentence
and I don't even know where it's going.
I just hope I find it along the way.

Kevin's chili recipe

People love my chili. Because it is the best chili. I like to make my chili for 20 people at least. I mix it all up at my house. I cook it overnight in a big pot and then drive it to the office in my car. I usually don't like to cook. I like to get home, put my feet up and get something delivered. Then I watch 14 hours of TV. Then I go to bed. I guess I would describe my perfect meal as sitting on the beach eating hot dogs. I also love Mexican food. The problem is, every time I try to make a taco I just get too excited and crush it.

Here is my chili recipe.

◇◇

Ingredients

10 big onions

1 cup cooking oil

6 pounds ground beef

15 tablespoons chili powder

8 tablespoons salt

6 tablespoons paprika

2 tablespoons ground red pepper

6 tablespoons Tabasco sauce

1 tablespoon oregano

5 cans diced tomatoes

3 cans concentrated tomato purée

6 cans red kidney beans

Method

Slice up the onions and fry them in hot oil until they become tender.

Add the meat, sprinkled with chili powder, salt, paprika, red pepper, Tabasco sauce and oregano.

Brown the meat.

Add the tomatoes and the concentrated tomato purée. Simmer, covered, for 50 minutes. Top up with water if it dries out.

Add the beans and simmer for another 20 minutes.

Take it into work as a treat – but you gotta be real careful carrying the heavy pot over carpeted areas.

A DAY IN THE LIFE OF
Jan Levinson

6.00 am: Woken up by Michael moving my wine glasses as he leaves the bedroom. Why can't he be more quiet when he makes up his cot at the base of the bed?

6.10 am: Fall asleep listening to Michael complete his pre-work vocal warm-ups in the kitchen. He's filled the house with a pungent bacon smell. Note to Jan: throw the George Foreman Grill in the trash when he leaves today.

10.00 am: Wake up to the sound of delivery man knocking at the door. My candle supplies have arrived! I shout out of the bedroom window for him to leave it on the porch. Time for more sleep.

10.55 am: Get out of bed.

11.15 am: Take a shower, lit only by Serenity by Jan candles.

12.00 pm: Get out of shower.

12.20 pm: Change into sweatpants and drive Michael's car to yoga. I pass by Chili's on the way to grab something to go. They've got a special on – a two-for-one deal on lemon margaritas and margarita glasses filled with shrimp. Order two of each and take a booth.

1.00 pm: Skip my yoga class and stop for cigarettes instead.

1.10 pm: Remember that I've left the candles lit in the bathroom from my shower earlier.

1.30 pm: Return home to put out the fire in the bathroom. Luckily only Michael's things got damaged.

2.00 pm: Pour myself a big glass of wine, light some candles and listen to Hunter's CD.

3.30 pm: Dinner time. Was planning on cooking but end up ordering in Chinese food on Michael's credit card.

4.30 pm: Enjoy a couple more glasses of wine. Michael will be home in an hour.

5.30 pm: Bed time!

SEASON 7
overview

We rejoin the team to find that Erin and Gabe have started a relationship over the summer break, despite Erin's hesitations. Andy is not happy about it and sets about winning her affections, including landing a role in the local production of *Sweeney Todd* and inviting everyone in the office to come along. Michael's wish comes true when Holly returns to replace Toby while he's on jury duty. Michael finds out that Holly and AJ have broken up after Holly gave him a marriage ultimatum. Shortly after they start dating again, Michael decides to propose to Holly himself. He tries to come up with the most extravagant proposal imaginable, armed with a stunning diamond ring that costs what he believes is the traditional "three years' salary." After consulting with other members of the office and being talked down from dangerous proposal ideas including fire and gasoline, he leads Holly into an office filled with their teammates holding candles, which results in the fire sprinklers going off above them. Holly says yes.

Not long after, Michael and Holly move to Boulder together. Steve Carell's departure from the show was significant, with many critics believing it would spell the end for *The Office*. After Michael's departure Jo appoints Deangelo Vickers – whom she met when he saved one of her dogs from being stolen – as the new regional manager. The team is unimpressed with Deangelo's "motivational" mimed juggling act. He is injured in a fluke accident during a Nerf basketball match and is sent to hospital. He later reappears in the office dressed in a hospital smock and speaking nonsense. This is the last we see of Deangelo.

After Jim turns down Jo's offer to be Deangelo's replacement, she asks Dwight, who accepts. Moments later, in a meeting with Dwight she discovers that he keeps a loaded gun in the office, resulting in her asking him to step down immediately. Due to his "seniority," Creed is assigned the role of temporary regional manager while they seek out a permanent replacement. Erin realizes that she really doesn't like Gabe that much and they break up. Heartbroken, Gabe returns to Florida with Jo's blessing. Angela has become engaged to her new boyfriend, Robert, who she frequently mentions is a senator. Oscar and the rest of the office believe he is secretly gay. In *Search Committee*, the final episode of the season, Deangelo's new replacement is sought out through a committee process led by Jim. Gabe and Kelly compete for the role but the season ends with the role still unfilled.

THE HISTORY OF
Schrute Farms

In 1778, Dwide Schrude first arrived in Pennsylvania with his family, after making the 4000-mile journey by horse and buggy from their native Germany. Schrude did not care for the larger and more glamorous American cities like New York City or Chicago and he also wanted to avoid the war in the South. His simple dream was to settle his family among the inhospitable summer humidity and sub-freezing winters that the Pennsylvania climate offered. Legend has it that in his first year in Scranton, Schrude planted and harvested beets for 19 hours a day, the whole family sleeping amongst his 60 acres of barren land with only a corn shuck each to rest upon at night.

The first Schrude Farms beet harvest was a great success and, with the money they made selling the beets in the local market, Schrude began the lengthy job of building a nine-bedroom, one-bathroom home for his two wives and 11 children out of Pennsylvanian swamp maple. He constructed the family bathroom under the front porch to save space, with occupants needing to climb through a hatch in the floor in order to enter.

Disaster struck at the end of the first summer when the house was burned to the ground after a family evacuation exercise that went wrong. A passionate survivalist, Schrude was an early adopter of what we now call fire drills. While he was counting his wives and children outside, a burning candle inside the house fell into a vat of beet liquor and the home was soon engulfed by flames. Schrude was badly injured in the fire and remained bedridden for the rest of his life. The house was entirely rebuilt by the Schrude children as the wives had to walk 40 miles into town each day to sell the remaining summer beets. The oldest Schrude boy, Dwight, took over the home and changed the family name to Schrute. By 1800, the Schrute Beet Farm was fully rebuilt, and became the state's thirtieth-most prolific grower of root vegetables – an accolade it holds to this day.

SCHRUTE FARMS TRIPADVISOR REVIEWS

"I didn't like the owner too much. He told me I was being rude when I asked for extra blankets. He had us sleeping in a barn in the middle of January. When they advertised that they used 200-year-old mattresses I thought they were joking. Turns out they weren't." – SuperNovak

"One morning I woke up and there was a skunk asleep in my suitcase. When I complained to the owner he offered me a full refund providing I was able to beat him in a foot race across the beet plantation. When I declined, he sent another man with a long beard to chase me from the farm with a pitchfork." – GreggyD

"I could hear crying from my room at night. Also my room smelled a lot like beets." – BigSchur

"The pillows were stuffed with straw. When I asked if I could heat up my baby's bottle of formula, the owner said he didn't believe in it and poured it down the sink. He offered us goat's milk as a replacement." – Mindy79

"The owner's cousin appeared to be in a sexual relationship with a scarecrow." – Kohkoh

"We were promised a traditional Pennsylvanian banquet but I don't think possum is a traditional dish around here. I found a bunch of bullet casings and shot pellets in my meal, but they were somehow only in the vegetables, not the meat." – MerchantofVenice

"Something bit my wife on the leg in our room on the third night. When we asked for assistance, the owner suggested that someone called 'Mose' would 'suck the venom out.' We left in the middle of the night without paying the check." – GetBrent69

"The architecture reminds one of a quaint Tuscan beet farm, and the natural aroma of the beets drifts into the bedrooms and makes you dream of simpler times. You will never want to leave your room. The informative lecture will satisfy all your beet curiosity, and the dawn goose walk will tug at your heart strings. Table making never seemed so possible. Great story to tell your friends. Plenty of parking! The staff's attention to detail and devotion to cleanliness was limitless. From their enthusiastic welcome to the last wave good-bye, Schrute Farms delivers." – JandP2

THE DUNDIES

5/03   20:55

15

Your Account Stated to Date-If Error Is Found Return a...

The Dundies is the annual employee awards ceremony hosted by Michael Scott. We first attend The Dundies in the first episode of Season 2 and then again in *Michael's Last Dundies* at the end of Season 7. Though the awards are meant to celebrate the employees of Dunder Mifflin, they are all chosen by Michael Scott and often insulting to the recipient. The venue of choice is the local Chili's, Michael's favorite restaurant. Michael also uses The Dundies to showcase his singing and comedic talents, much to the confusion of people seated nearby.

Michael has taped every Dundie awards although it is highly unlikely that anyone else has ever watched them. As Oscar puts it, "The Dundies are kind of like a kid's birthday party. And you go, and there's really nothing for you to do there, but the kid's having a really good time, so you ... You're kind of there. That's ... That's kind of what it's like." When Michael Scott leaves Scranton, he insists that the annual awards continue, stating, "The Dundies are my baby and they need to go on." He co-hosts with Deangelo Vickers who finds the responsibility overwhelming.

Some of the most memorable Dundies awarded:

Phyllis: Busiest Beaver Award (misspelled as Bushiest Beaver)

Ryan: Hottest in the Office 2005, 2006, 2007, 2008, 2009 and 2010

Angela: Tight-ass Award

Kevin: Don't Go in There After Me

Stanley: Fine Work Award

Pam: Whitest Sneakers Award

Stanley: Diabetes Award

Andy: Doobie Doobie Pothead Stoner of the Year Award

Toby: Extreme Repulsiveness Award

Phyllis: Redefining Beauty Award

Angela: Kind of a Bitch Award

Darryl: Moving On Up Award

Oscar: Worst Salesman of the Year

In the first completely Michael Scott–free season of *The Office*, we see the appointment of the mysterious Robert California. Recently divorced, Robert is obsessed with the primal desires of humans and aligns them with how he does business. Jo hires him as regional manager, but on his first day he takes a look around the office and drives straight back to Florida to demand the role of CEO. This leaves Andy in the coveted role of regional manager. Pam is pregnant again after a romantic Valentine's Day with Jim. Angela is also with child, having married Robert the Senator over the summer break. But there is soon trouble in paradise when we learn that Robert is cheating on Angela with Oscar. The warehouse staff win $450,000 in the lottery and resign, forcing some of the office team to work there until replacements are found.

In *Tallahassee,* some of the team head to Florida to work on a special project, which is where we meet Nellie Bertram, President of Special Projects. Nellie is British, very blunt and not entirely convincing as a leader. She sells the idea of the Sabre Retail Store, based very closely on Apple stores, where they will sell the triangular tablet computer, "The Pyramid." As advertised on the Sabre website, it claims to be "Your portable connection to everything in space and time." However, it is clearly a poorly designed device and is not yet able to connect to wifi internet.

Dwight is keen to impress Nellie in Florida but is struck down with appendicitis. Cathy, the temp filling in for Pam, makes a move on Jim at the hotel, while Nellie makes a move on Dwight. Dwight and Jim both rebuke the women's advances and hide out in a hotel together on a bed eating desserts. Upon their return to Scranton, Dwight is made VP of Sabre retail under Nellie. Robert California ends up tanking the store, putting Dwight and Nellie's jobs in jeopardy. In *Jury Duty*, Angela gives birth "prematurely" to a very large baby at 9 lb 7 oz. The visitors from the office are shocked, and Dwight declares that Philip "is a Schrute, and unless someone taught Mose sex, that baby is mine."

Inspired by the Tallahassee trip, Erin decides to leave Scranton and move to Florida as a live-in helper for an elderly lady. Andy decides to go to her and declare his love, leaving his post as manager of Scranton. In *Get the Girl*, Nellie craftily travels to the Scranton

Continued >>

branch, and decides that, with Andy away in Florida, it is the perfect opportunity to steal his job. When Andy returns with Erin and tries to wrestle his job back, Nellie deploys a series of tactics to break his confidence. There is a violent outburst from Andy where he throws his chair at Robert California and punches through a wall, resulting in him being demoted.

In the final episode of Season 8, *Free Family Portrait Studio,* Andy is finally appointed Regional Manager again, after David Wallace purchases Dunder Mifflin from Sabre with the $20 million that he made from selling a toy vacuum invention to the military. Nellie begs Andy to show her mercy despite her bad behavior toward him, and he decides to re-hire her as a special projects manager. Robert California is also departing Scranton. He has convinced David to bankroll his charity, for which he will be traveling the world educating and mentoring women, seeing them right through college, "especially the gymnasts." Dwight steals a nappy from Angela's baby to use for a paternity test. However, we will have to wait until Season 9 to learn the results.

0188451

Date _____ 20 ____

M _____

No. _____

Reg. No.	Clerk	ACCOUNT FORWARD		
1				
2				
3				
4				
5				
6				

An employee will go home and he'll tell his neighbor, "Hey, did you get an award?" And the neighbor will say, "no man. I mean I slave all day and no one notices me." Next thing you know, employee smells something terrible coming from the neighbor's house. neighbor's hanged himself, due to lack of recognition.

THE OFFICE
Top 10 episodes

Halloween
Season 2, Episode 5

The office is all set to celebrate Halloween, with Dwight dressed as a Sith Lord, Creed as Dracula, Kelly as Dorothy from *The Wizard of Oz* and Kevin in an extremely tight-fitting red suit from *The Incredibles*. Michael has attached a second head made of papier mâché to his shoulder, and is enjoying the day until he remembers that Jan has asked him to fire someone from the branch to cut costs.

Michael agonizes over the decision, and tries to hand off the responsibility to almost everyone else in the office. The absurdity of a boss asking his staff to decide who he should fire is made even more ridiculous by everyone being in costume as the drama unfolds. Eventually Michael decides to fire Creed, who outsmarts him into firing Devon instead. Devon retaliates by inviting everyone but Michael out for a drink, and then throwing a jack-o'-lantern onto Michael's car. At the end of the episode we see Michael leaving the office, mournfully cleaning off his car and then watching television in his condo alone. Some trick or treaters knock on the door and he sweetly offers them a very generous amount of candy.

Best moment

Michael offers Devon a Chili's gift certificate in addition to his severance.

Best quote

Dwight: "Would I ever leave this company? Look, I'm all about loyalty. In fact, I feel like part of what I'm being paid for here is my loyalty. But if there were somewhere else that valued loyalty more highly, I'm going wherever they value loyalty the most."

Casino Night
Season 2, Episode 22

Michael organizes a casino night in the warehouse to raise money for charity and ends up inviting two "dates" – Jan Levinson and Carol his real estate agent. Pam has been planning her wedding to Roy, but most of her happiness seems to come from the fact that she has been spending time with Jim, choosing bands to play at the wedding. Jim is less optimistic about the future and meets with Jan to discuss transferring to the Stamford office, because he "has no future here."

Roy leaves the party early, leaving Pam and Jim simmering over a game of poker. When Jan realizes that Michael has chosen to woo Carol for the evening, she drives home to New York, feeling rejected and foolish. Jim later admits his feelings for Pam in the parking lot, to which Pam heartbreakingly responds, "I can't. I'm really sorry if you misinterpreted things." Later, they kiss in the office in full view of the documentary cameras.

Best moment

When Dwight rolls an 8 in a game of craps and in excitement he kisses Angela on the cheek. She immediately slaps him hard on the face. He is shocked, but she walks away, titillated.

Best quote

Michael: [to Toby] "Why are you the way that you are? Honestly, every time I try to do something fun or exciting, you make it not … that way. I hate so much about the things that you choose to be."

Launch Party
Season 4, Episodes 5/6

Michael announces that he and Jim are off to New York to attend the launch party for the *Dunder Mifflin Infinity* website. The rest of the office staff aren't invited but will be tuning in via a webcam. Dwight challenges the website to make more sales than him, so Jim and Pam pretend to be the website contacting Dwight through his computer, mocking him. The website is clearly beating Dwight and he becomes frustrated when existing clients start using it to re-order paper. As they cross the state line, Michael reads out the invite and Jim realizes it was just for the online party. Michael was never invited.

Jim and Michael return to the office and Michael asks Angela to arrange a list of outrageous party demands. Michael orders pizza for the office party and tries to pay the delivery boy with coupons. When the boy will not accept them, Michael takes him hostage in the conference room. The live cross from New York begins, and they introduce Michael Scott, who calls Ryan an a**hole in front of the whole company. Michael realizes the gravity of the kidnapping situation when the pizza boy sends a message via the webcam saying he is being held against his will. They let him go.

Best moment

Pam and Jim escape the party to sit on the rooftop on deckchairs eating pizza, reminiscing about the moments they first knew they liked each other.

Best quote

Michael: [about the pizza boy kidnapping] "You don't even know what stupid is – it's about to get all stupid up in here."

The Deposition
Season 4, Episode 12

Michael is to be deposed in New York as part of Jan's $4 million wrongful termination lawsuit. Michael bumbles through the deposition, unable to resist bad jokes and stumbles over his rehearsed lines. Jan produces Michael's personal diary, from which they read a highly embarrassing entry, which proves that despite them sleeping together in Jamaica, she did not believe they were in a relationship.

It is also revealed that Jan has given Michael poor performance reviews even after they got together and that David Wallace never saw him as a contender for the corporate job despite referring to him as a "nice guy." But Michael refuses to say that Dunder Mifflin did the wrong thing, to Jan's frustration. Her case is lost.

Best moment

David takes Michael aside to apologize. Michael has chosen to focus on David saying he was a nice guy. Michael explains "David, I think you're a nice guy too ... you expect to get screwed by your company but you never expect to get screwed by your girlfriend."

Best quote

Jan's Lawyer: [reading from Michael's journal] "I quote from an entry dated January four of this past year. 'Just got back from Jamaica. Tan almost everywhere. Jan almost everywhere. Hee hee. Oh diary, what a week. I had sex with my boss. I don't know if it's going to go anywhere. Jan was very specific that this is not going anywhere, that it was a one-time mistake. But we had sex six times so you tell me. I am definitely feeling very eerie.'"

Dinner Party
Season 4, Episode 13

Not only is *Dinner Party* regarded by many fans as the show's finest episode, it is arguably one of the funniest episodes of any sitcom ever. Michael talks the office staff into working late on a Friday by pretending that corporate have told him to do so, just to trick Jim and Pam into coming to dinner. Andy and Angela also get invited but Dwight misses out as it's "couples only" and he doesn't have enough glasses. Dwight shows up halfway through the night anyway, with an elderly woman he claims to be his former babysitter. They bring their own wine glasses and cooler of food.

The tension between Michael and Jan is excruciating as they navigate their first dinner party as a couple, fumbling on every step and exposing the flaws in their relationship to their horrified co-workers, referring to each other as "babe" and "honey" through gritted teeth. This escalates to Jan throwing one of Michael's Dundies at his $200 plasma TV. The police are called and Dwight takes Michael to stay at his house for the night, while Jan mournfully glues the Dundie statuette back together.

Best moment

Jan puts on a CD of her former assistant Hunter's band and dances sensually in front of the guests. The lyrics of the song clearly imply that Hunter lost his virginity to an older woman, most likely Jan.

Best quote

Michael: "You have no idea the physical toll that three vasectomies have on a person."

Stress Relief
Season 5, Episodes 14/15

In one of the funniest cold opens in TV history, Dwight holds a fire drill involving realistic special effects such as multiple heated door knobs, firecrackers and smoke. A mass panic ensues, culminating in Stanley having a heart attack. When he eventually returns to the office, Michael decides to run a "stress relief" session for the office. However, it soon becomes clear to everyone that he is in fact the source of most of the stress in the branch.

Bafflingly, Michael invites the team to "roast" him that night in the warehouse as a solution to their stress. After a particularly scathing roast from Dwight, and Pam mentioning his small penis, Michael becomes increasingly sad and has to leave the party. He even takes a personal day the following day. When Michael shows up at the end of the day, the team are apologetic. Michael decides to roast the team himself, however his method is simply to insult each person individually followed by the words "Boom, roasted." The office erupts in laughter and Michael leaves on top of the world, feeling that he has "cured" Stanley.

Best moment

Angela panics and throws her cat, Bandit, through a gap in the ceiling demanding that Oscar save him as he escapes. The cat flies up into the ceiling cavity and promptly falls back down through another panel.

Best quote

Meredith: "Michael, you are the reason I drink. You are the reason I live to forget."

Moroccan Christmas
Season 5, Episode 11

It is Phyllis' first Christmas party as head of the Party Planning Committee. She chooses the theme "Nights in Morocco," making Angela do all of the heavy lifting in exchange for her not telling Andy she is cheating on him with Dwight. Meredith has too many cocktails and, while drunkenly dancing, her hair catches on fire and Dwight puts it out with an extinguisher. Michael decides to stage an intervention for Meredith during the party as he is worried that she is an alcoholic.

This culminates in Michael attempting to check Meredith into a rehabilitation facility against her will, which she violently fights against. When the facility will not accept Meredith as she has to do it voluntarily, Michael drives her home. Meanwhile, Angela is fed up with Phyllis and refuses to do any more work. This leads to Phyllis announcing to the team "Angela is having sex with Dwight, I caught them doing it after Toby's going away party" to which Dwight slyly replies, "Well don't look so surprised."

Best moment

Andy plays "Deck the Halls" on the sitar for the party, oblivious to the fact that Angela and Dwight's affair has just been revealed to the rest of the office. He comments on the "tough crowd" as he leaves with a silent Angela.

Best quote

Michael: "Meredith, you lit your hair on fire today. What about tomorrow? What is going to happen when you come into work and you're dead?"

Threat Level Midnight
Season 7, Episode 17

"After three years of writing, one year of shooting, four years of re-shooting and two years of editing" Michael has finally completed his movie, *Threat Level Midnight*. He screens the film for the whole office, wanting to impress Holly. This episode is enjoyable not only because Michael's film utilizes every movie cliché in the book, but also that it was shot by Michael a few years earlier, so we get to see some of the cast who have since left Scranton, like Karen and Jan.

The movie tells the story of Michael Scarn, once the "best secret agent in the business" whose wife, Catherine Zeta Scarn, was brutally murdered. Scarn retires to become a paper salesman, but is soon called on by the President of the United States to take down his enemy "Goldenface," who has taken a bunch of people hostage inside a hockey stadium. The audience is treated to Michael Scarn completing a hockey training montage and an inexplicable choreographed dance routine in a bar called "Do the Scarn."

Best moment

Goldenface shoots Toby's character in the head in an incredibly violent scene replayed over and over again in the film. Michael says it is "far and away the most expensive shot in the movie but it was integral to the story" because Toby's character was a "wanted animal rapist."

Best quote

Michael Scarn: "It's going to take a lot more than a bullet to the brain, lungs, heart, back and balls to kill Michael Scarn!"

Garage Sale
Season 7, Episode 19

The office holds a garage sale. Michael has decided he wants to propose to Holly that day, and leaves a voicemail with her dad asking for his permission. On a whim, he decides to propose using words written in burning gasoline in the parking lot. However, luckily Pam stops him, saying, "Michael, you've had two ideas today. And one of them was great and the other one was terrible." Jim, Oscar, Ryan and Pam take Michael into the conference room to come up with ideas for a more safe proposal. When Pam sees the ring, which Michael has spent three years' salary on, she tells him, "I think you can keep the proposal simple."

Later that day, Michael leads Holly on a tour of the office, pointing out all the places where they had special moments together. They walk into the annex and each member of the office is holding a candle. They all ask her to marry them one by one and she says no to each of them. The fire sprinklers start going off, soaking Michael and Holly. Michael gets down on one knee and proposes to Holly in his "Yoda" voice. She says yes in her "Yoda" voice and they kiss.

Best moment

Dwight swaps his $150 telescope for a packet of "Magic legumes" that Jim is selling at the garage sale. At the end of the episode, Dwight plants the seeds and Jim secretly replaces the pots with fully grown plants.

Best quote

Michael: "How about this; I throw a corpse dressed like me off the roof. It hits the ground and the head pops off. And this leads to me saying the line 'I lost my head when I fell in love with you.' And it's easy to get a corpse these days, right? Just call the local medical college."

Pool Party
Season 8, Episode 12

Robert California is selling his palatial home after his divorce, and the whole office are invited over for a pool party. Erin is trying to get over Andy who has a new girlfriend, Jessica. His parents have given Andy an old family ring to propose to her with, though his mother has taken the biggest diamond out. Robert is walking around in lounge wear and takes a group of the men from the office on a tour, discussing his disappointments about the house and his marriage along the way. After Andy rebuffed Erin's flirting, Erin and Dwight try to make Andy and Angela jealous by flirting in the pool, staging multiple "chicken fights" that get increasingly violent.

Andy loses the engagement ring, which Erin eventually finds. When she gives it to Andy, he tells her he doesn't know what he is doing with Jessica and Erin is thrilled. Robert's tour returns to the pool, significantly drunker than when they set off. Robert looks around the room at the group enjoying themselves and decides to jump into the pool naked, to "mourn the nights that never were." Gabe and Ryan strip naked too and join him. Jim interprets this as a good time to leave.

Best moment

Very late in the night, Robert, Gabe and Ryan dance in the house under psychedelic lights. Robert tells them, "It's not a party if you don't do something that scares you" then falls asleep in a chair. Gabe and Ryan have the perfect opportunity to escape, yet they both choose to remain dancing, presumably late into the night.

Best quote

Gabe: [interrupting Ryan trying to bond with Robert on his own] "And Gabey makes three."

Wikipedia is the best thing ever. Anyone in the world can write anything they want about any subject. So you know you are getting the best possible information.

SEASON 9
overview

In *New Guys*, Kevin introduces us to the final season and gives us a recap of the summer, reporting that he has run over a turtle with his car. Kelly has left for Ohio with her pediatrician fiancé and Ryan is mysteriously also heading to Ohio, claiming it is the "other" Silicon Valley. We learn that one of Jim's friends is starting a sports marketing company in Philadelphia based on an idea they came up with together. However, Jim has chosen to stay in Scranton with Pam. There are two new junior members of the office, Pete ("The New Jim") and Clark ("Dwight Junior"). Angela has told Dwight that baby Philip is not his, and remains married to Robert.

Andy has made Darryl Philbin from the warehouse his assistant regional manager and becomes focussed on getting rid of unpopular Nellie for good. Oscar's affair with Angela's husband Robert is revealed to us on camera in *The Boat* when we see them kissing. Kevin witnesses them embracing passionately while he is eating an ice cream nearby. When Oscar realizes, he tries to get Kevin to keep the secret, which proves difficult. Eventually Jim re-joins the business venture with his friend but keeps it from Pam.

Darryl is sick of life at Dunder Mifflin, as is Jim. Jim talks to him about the opportunities at his company in Philadelphia and breaks the news to Pam. She isn't mad about the job opportunity, more that he kept it from her. This forms a rift in Jim and Pam's relationship, which gets worse when the effects of Jim's absence set in, while he works in Philadelphia part-time.

Angela tells Oscar that she suspects Robert is cheating on her, and takes Oscar on a spy mission. This leads to her discovering that Oscar is the one her husband is cheating with when Oscar's phone rings during a stakeout, and it is Robert who is calling. Angela messes with Oscar, and he is unsure if she actually knows or not. In the meantime, Angela is planning to have Oscar killed and goes to Dwight for advice on a hitman. When the hit is about to be made, Dwight realizes that Oscar is the planned victim and tries to stop it. This results in a confrontation between Angela and Oscar. Finally the truth is out.

Andy's family loses all their money so he decides to go to the Bahamas to sell his family's boat. This becomes a three-month trip, with Andy lying to

Continued >>

David that he is still in the office. Erin gets closer to Pete in Andy's absence. Jim and Pam begin to fight more when they are together. We meet Brian, a boom operator from the documentary crew, who has begun to get closer to Pam. One of the warehouse staff vandalizes Pam's mural and she takes revenge by vandalizing his truck. The man gets aggressive with Pam and Brian intervenes, resulting in Brian getting fired.

Robert continues to stay married to Angela while having an affair with Oscar. At a birthday celebration for baby Philip, which is a poorly veiled political stunt for the senator, both Angela and Oscar realize they are being used. Dwight has moved on with a local brussels sprout farmer named Esther. Andy returns from his three-month trip in a disheveled state and Erin breaks up with him.

The TV premiere of the documentary *The Office: An American Workplace* is imminent, so Robert decides to announce in a press conference that he is gay. Robert and Angela divorce soon after, leaving her depressed and in poverty. She admits to Oscar that she needs help and is still in love with Dwight. Oscar feels guilty so he invites her and Philip to live with him. Jim takes a break from his new job to spend more time in Scranton. David promotes Dwight to Regional Manager after being inspired by his choice to sit for his black belt exam in his favorite place in the world, the office. Andy is demoted to salesman and Jim is given the role of Assistant to the Regional Manager.

Dwight confronts Angela about Philip's real father, and offers Angela his hand in marriage if the test proves that he is. Jim gives Dwight a pep talk to admit to himself that he loves Angela and they are meant to be together. Dwight chases Angela in his car to propose marriage and Angela says yes. In the second-last episode of *The Office*, the team all meet at a local bar to watch the first episode of the documentary.

I feel like all my kids grew up,
and then they married each other.
It's every parent's dream!

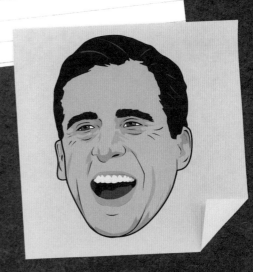

More than five million people tuned in for *Finale*, the hour-long last episode of *The Office*. We learn that PBS have screened the *The Office: An American Workplace* series and have sent a crew to follow up with the team one year later so that they can compile some extras for the planned DVD release. We find that Dwight has had a successful year as the manager of the Scranton branch, instating Japanese business practices such as exercising before work. He is also days away from marrying Angela. He informs us that there have been some changes in staff. Stanley has retired and Dwight has fired Toby and Kevin, using a cake to celebrate each. Jim is going to be Dwight's "Bestest Mensch" for the wedding, and has been charged with organizing his bachelor party, which will involve several "Guten Pranken" (good pranks). We find out that Creed faked his own death in the warehouse baler and is on the run from the law. Oscar is running for senator and Stanley has retired to the Florida everglades.

Former Dunder Mifflin employees begin to arrive in Scranton for Dwight and Angela's wedding and to participate in a panel discussion about the documentary. Darryl and Andy arrive at the airport at the same time. Darryl is taken away in a private car while Andy waits at the taxi rank. Darryl now lives in Austin and is enjoying his success. Andy's sobbing performance on a TV talent show has gone viral, and he now works in admissions at Cornell. Nellie lives in Poland now, "the Scranton of the EU," and Toby has moved to New York to write the "great American novel," though we get the impression this sounds more romantic than it is.

At Dwight's bachelor party, Jim's plans get off to a good start when the limo stops in a field where Dwight is invited to fire a bazooka. The group arrive at a Bavarian-themed restaurant where a buxom stripper appears. Dwight mistakenly believes she is a waitress and requests an onion loaf for the table and for her to tell them about their heartiest soups. Meanwhile at Angela's bachelorette party we meet her socially awkward sister. The stripper arrives, dressed as a generic "repairman," and it turns out to be Meredith's son. An uncomfortable routine ensues. Angela hears noises outside and asks Phyllis to lock the door. While Phyllis is doing so, Mose Schrute kidnaps Angela.

Continued >>

When Dwight is told of this, he is thrilled as kidnapping the wife is a traditional prank in his family. In the tradition, Mose will deliver her to a local bar. When they arrive at the bar, they find that Kevin now owns it and he tries to throw Dwight out. Eventually they reminisce about the past and hug. The group has forgotten about Angela, who has been locked in the trunk of a car the whole time. She is not happy.

The following day it is time for the panel discussion. The group arrives to a very small audience, which upsets Andy. He soon realizes that a huge crowd of fans have turned up, just for him. Many audience members question Pam about Jim's choice to leave his new career behind and stay with her in Scranton. In a heartwarming moment, Erin's long-lost mother and father reveal themselves to her and they embrace. As the audience applauds the end of the discussion, we see that Creed is hiding in the audience sporting a long beard.

At Dwight and Angela's wedding day, the guests begin to arrive and many place cats in a basket as gifts. Kelly is attending with her pediatrician husband. Ryan shows up with his baby and we learn that the mother has left them after claiming she was popping out for an e-cigarette charger. Just before the ceremony, Jim gives Dwight the bad news. The priest has informed him that the "Bestest Mensch" needs to be older than the groom. Dwight is crestfallen, until Jim introduces his replacement ... Michael Scott. Dwight is overjoyed and exclaims, "Michael, I can't believe you came." "That's what she said" is Michael's reply, and the two embrace.

As is traditional at Schrute weddings, the lovers are standing in their own graves to remind each other that this is the only escape from what they are about to do. Romantic sparks fly between Kelly and Ryan, culminating in Ryan giving the baby an allergic reaction to a strawberry so that he can be alone with Kelly. They kiss passionately and leave the wedding together. Ryan's baby ends up in the care of Nellie, who makes her intentions clear. She will be taking the baby with her to Poland.

Michael shows Pam that he has two cell phones full of photos of the children he has had with Holly. Now that Dwight and Angela are married as well as

Jim and Pam, Michael says that he feels "like all my kids grew up and they married each other. It's every parent's dream." The team head over to the warehouse for an after party put on by the documentary makers. Jim and Pam return home and Pam's real estate agent mom is there selling the house. Pam tells Jim that she wants to sell the house and move the family to Austin for his career. They embrace and back at the after party, they announce the news to Darryl who is ecstatic.

At the party, Pam reveals a large mural, *The History of Us*, showing all of the members of the office over the years. The office gang decide to escape the PBS executives and head into the office for a final drink together. Upon learning of their intention to resign, Dwight fires Pam and Jim so that they can get severance payouts. The team gather around Darryl's computer to watch Andy's Cornell speech. It is revealed that Creed is living in the men's room. He plays a sentimental song on his guitar as they enjoy their final moments together in the office. Pam takes her framed drawing of the office off the wall as they leave.

After 201 episodes, *The Office* ends with our favorite characters describing how being part of the documentary has altered them. Andy reflects on how things have changed since and wishes for "a way to know you were in the good old days before you have actually left them."

Pam leaves us with perfect parting words: "There is a lot of beauty in ordinary things, isn't that kind of the point?"

5/03   20:55

15

Your Account Stated to Date-If Error Is Found Return at

It's hard to believe that *The Office* ended in 2013. However, thanks to streaming and TV repeats, the Dunder Mifflin fandom grows more and more each day. In many ways *The Office* paved the way for modern sitcoms like *Parks and Recreation* and *Brooklyn 99*. It showed us that it's okay to have the intimate relationships of the characters at the center of the story, rather than just using them as a vehicle for one-liners. It also further proved that we don't need a laugh track to tell us what is funny.

Popular TV show reboots in recent times, like *Will & Grace, Roseanne* and *Twin Peaks* have inspired many *Office* fans to ponder the possibility of an *Office* reunion. In so many ways, *Finale* was the perfect end for the show, with so many characters moving on from Dunder Mifflin. Though some of the cast seem to be open to the idea of a reunion, Steve Carell has said, "The show is way more popular now than when it was on the air. I just can't see it being the same thing, and I think most folks would want it to be the same thing, but it wouldn't be. Ultimately, I think it's maybe best to leave well enough alone and just let it exist as what it was."

In 2018, *Saturday Night Live* staged a reunion of some of the stars of *The Office* when Steve Carell was guest hosting. Jenna Fischer, Ed Helms and Ellie Kemper appeared in the opening monologue to ask Carell to join them in a reunion, which he politely declines. *The Office* also goes on in social media with thousands of Facebook, Reddit and Instagram accounts devoted to sharing *Office* memes and GIFs. We can also follow many of our favorite stars of the show on their personal Instagram accounts and enjoy their occasional reunions with each other.

What *The Office* meant to all of us is personal. If you work in an office every day, look around you. There is probably a Jim, a Kevin, a Michael or an Angela. But be warned. If you look around and can't find him, maybe the Dwight Schrute of your office is you.

Don't worry, I know that might be hard to swallow.

That's what she said.

TRIVIA

How well do you know The Office?

(Questions)

1. What is the name of Kevin Malone's Police cover band?

2. What is the name of Angela's cat that she had to give away when her baby, Philip, developed an allergy?

3. What were the names of the "identical" waitresses who Michael Scott met at Benihana?

4. What is the name of Jo Bennett's autobiography?

5. What items does Jim place inside the teapot that he gives Pam for Secret Santa, apart from the note?

6. What disease is it revealed that Kevin suffers from in *Health Care*?

7. What Dundie does Michael Scott award Ryan when he starts as a temp?

8. Which member of the office did Michael Scott go to school with?

9. What is the name of Hunter's single?

10. What does Michael eat in *Survivor Man* that results in Dwight rescuing him?

11. How many years was Pam engaged to Roy?

12. Who were the original members of The Finer Things Club?

13. What prized possession of Michael's does Jan destroy in *Dinner Party*?

14. What is Pam's mom's name?

15. What is the name of Erin's character in the Murder Mystery game in the episode *Murder*?

16. How did former Scranton branch manager Ed Truck die?

17. What branch did Karen Filippelli go on to manage after leaving Scranton?

18. What parody do Holly and Michael put on in the episode *Company Picnic*?

19. What is Angela's nickname for Dwight?

20. What is the stock symbol for Dunder Mifflin?

◇◇

Trivia answers

1. Scrantonicity 2. Comstock 3. Nikki and Amy 4. *Take a Good Look* 5. A cassette, Boggle timer, sachet of hotsauce, mini golf pencil and a photo of Jim from his high school yearbook. 6. Anal fissures 7. Hottest in the Office 8. Phyllis 9. "That One Night" 10. Poisonous mushrooms 11. Three years 12. Pam, Oscar and Toby 13. A plasma TV 14. Helene 15. Naughty Nelly 16. He was allegedly decapitated in a truck accident 17. Utica 18. *SlumDunder Mifflinaire* 19. D 20. DMI

Smith Street Books

Published in 2019 by Smith Street Books
Melbourne | Australia
smithstreetbooks.com

ISBN: 978-1-925811-28-5

All rights reserved. No part of this book may be reproduced or transmitted by any person or entity, in any form or means, electronic or mechanical, including photocopying, recording, scanning or by any storage and retrieval system, without the prior written permission of the publishers and copyright holders.

Copyright illustrations © Chantel de Sousa
Copyright text © Amy Lewis
Copyright design © Smith Street Books

The moral rights of the author have been asserted.

CIP data is available from the National Library of Australia.

Publisher: Paul McNally
Project editor: Hannah Koelmeyer
Editor: Ariana Klepac
Design and layout: Stephanie Spartels
Illustration: Chantel de Sousa, The Illustration Room
Proofreader: Pam Dunne

Printed & bound in China by C&C Offset Printing Co., Ltd.

Book 105
10 9 8 7 6 5 4 3 2 1

Please note: This title is not affiliated with or endorsed in any way by the creators or copyright holders of *The Office*. We are just big fans. Please don't sue us.